AF219472

The best magic tricks for kids

By
Susanne Rennert

Bibliographic information of the German National Library:
The German National Library lists this publication in the
German National Bibliography; detailed data are availa-
ble on the Internet at http://dnb.dnb.de.

All games in this book have been carefully selected and
checked. Nevertheless, no guarantee can be given. Lia-
bility for personal injury, property damage and financial
loss are excluded.

www.die-zauberkiste.de

© 2021 Susanne Rennert
Illustrations: Susanne Rennert
Fotos: Martina Sherman, Susanne Rennert,
S 51 Pixabay
Cover: Heike Georgi

Production and publishing
BoD - Books on Demand, Norderstedt
ISBN 9783754344286

Content

Preface

As a child, I was fascinated the first time I saw a magician. I was amazed at how he could make all those colorful cloths appear and disappear.

Those were tricks, I was told. But for the life of me, I couldn't figure out how to do it. I couldn't get rid of the thought of wanting to learn it myself. So I got my first magic box when I was 9 years old. When I got older, I learned to play in theater and then I played in a touring theater. Along the way I learned magic tricks and practiced them. I discovered a magic store in Berlin. I decided to hold my first magic performances there. After my studies as a social pedagogue, I gave magic courses for children. I did that for 10 years. It was so much fun that I thought about passing on my knowledge in books. That's how this magic book was birthed, in which I wrote down all my experiences from my magic courses, so that you can also hold magic performances.

I wish you much fun and success

Susanne Rennert

The three golden rules of conjuring

The basic equipment of a conjurer includes the following three very important rules:

1. A magician must never reveal a trick to friends, parents or relatives.

2. Each trick must be performed only once in front of the same audience. The first time, the audience watches WHAT you do. The second time, the audience sees HOW you do it and can therefore more easily see the trick secret.

3. Every trick must be practiced carefully before it is performed. You must feel absolutely confident in everything you say or show. It is best to practice in front of a mirror.

1. Magic tricks

Going through a postcard

You have to cut the postcard with scissors so that you can crawl through it. It all depends on the way you cut it.

Materials: scissors, paper the size of a 15 cm x 10 cm postcard (Din A 6)

1. The paper is folded in the middle of the long side.

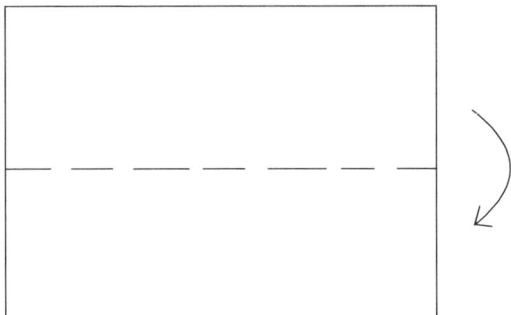

2. Now cut the paper alternately on the two short sides. Start on the side where the fold is located, about 1 cm from the edge. Cut the paper at a distance of 0.5 cm. The cuts should stop 1 cm before the end. This sounds complicated, but it is not. In the picture you will see how it is done.

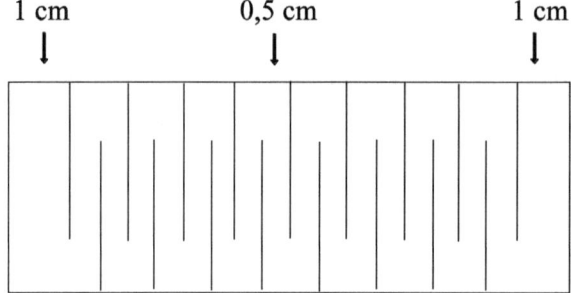

1 cm   0,5 cm   1 cm

3. The paper is unfolded again. It now consists of several strips of paper attached to each other. In the middle is the fold.

4. Finally, the fold is cut in the middle, avoiding the two end pieces. So only the bold Line is cut out. The result is a long circle of paper, through which you can pass loosely.

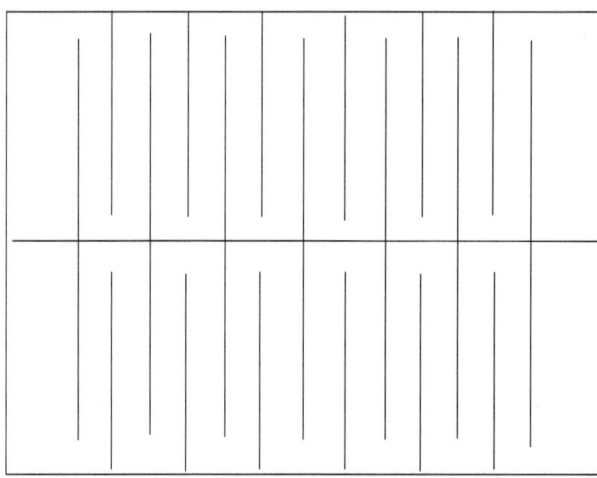

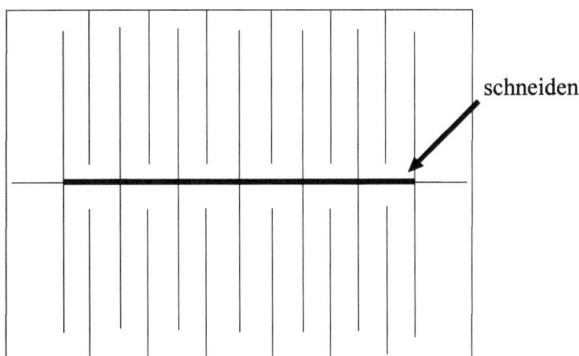

schneiden

5. The result is a long circle of paper, through which you can pass loosely.

The 3 magic rings

Materials: scissors, glue, 3 paper strips (each about 1.20 m long)

Preparation: Take 3 paper strips. They can be made from newspaper. On the first strip, glue the two ends together to form a ring. The third strip should be twisted twice before you glue it.

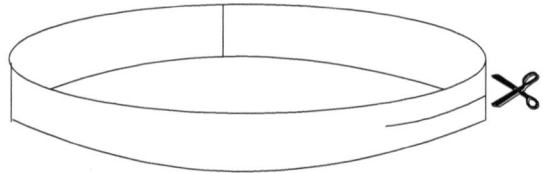

The second strip is twisted around itself once before gluing the ends together. The second strip is turned around once before taping the ends together.

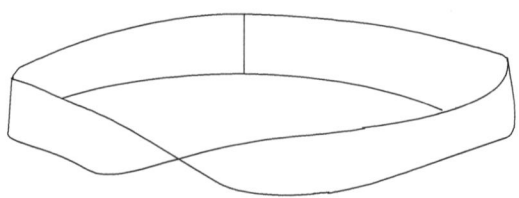

The third strip turns twice before you glue it.

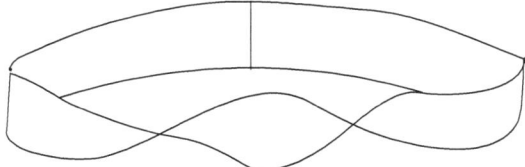

Demonstration: These rings are now ready to be demonstrated. Choose three assistants from the audience and ask them to join you on the playing area. Give each assistant a ring and a pair of scissors. To do this, take the strip in your hands so that the ring falls down nicely. Now cut the ring lengthwise in the middle.

Logically, 2 rings arise from the first ring. The once-twisted ring turns into a huge one and the twice-twisted one disintegrates into two small rings hanging inside each other. The assistants may sit down again.

By the way, the phenomenon of the bands has long been known in science as the "Möbius band".

Transforming a cloth into a ball

Materials:
Scissors, table tennis ball, a cloth made of silk, for example. The cloth can also be made of very thin material
such as taffeta fabric, which can be crumpled up and
made very small, about 25 cm x 25 cm.

Demonstration:
Step on stage and introduce yourself. Hold a cloth in
your hand and stuff it in with the other (as seen from the
audience).

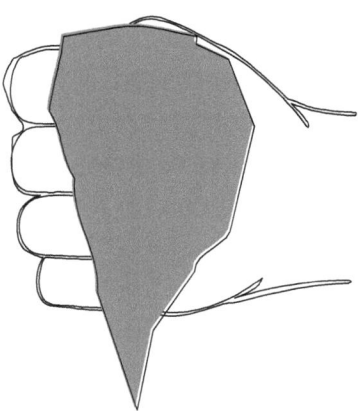

Once it has disappeared in your hand, make a magic
movement with the other one and cast a spell, e.g. Ho-
cus-pocus-Fidibus, three times black cat.
The hand is opened and the cloth has turned into a ping-
pong ball.

Explanation:
Of course, the ball is in the hand from the beginning. However, it has been prepared a bit beforehand. With a pair of pointed scissors, a hole that is big enough for your thumb to fit in is cut into it and you can stuff a cloth inside it.

When you step on stage, you have already "palmed" the ball in your hand. Palming means holding an object in your hand in such a way that the audience can't see or guess it. The ball is palmed in the inner palm of the hand, the so-called hand palm.

The back of the hand is turned towards the audience. The cloth hangs over the back of the hand. One end of the cloth is already in the hole of the ball. Everything is fixed with the thumb. The fingers are closed. There must be no gap through which the ball can be seen.
Now the cloth is stuffed into the ball until it disappears. The fingers of the other hand are placed on the hole to cover the opening.

The ball is shown so that the hole is turned away from the spectators. The magician bows and receives ap-plause.

The trick can't be performed if you tell what you are do-ing. You should be careful not to reveal what you are going to do. It is unwise to say that you are going to turn this cloth into a ball. The audience will pay close attention to see where the ball comes from. It is enough to explain the actions you are performing.

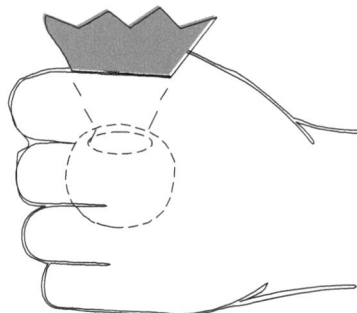

It is advantageous to let the audience actively participate in the action and to involve them. This could occur when you need some magic puff and the audience has to blow. I will go into this in more detail at a later time.

To follow your performance from the audience point of view, it is advisable to stand in front of a mirror and observe your actions.

The magic cocktail bar

4 glasses are filled with water and the water is magically colored.

Materials:
Table, 4 glasses, glass jug with water, 4 food dyes.

Demonstration:
"Good afternoon, my much honored audience. I am magician Pepito from the cocktail bar. Today I will show you my magic cocktail. But this will not be one cocktail, nor two cocktails, but four cocktails (takes a glass in one hand, the pitcher in the other).

First, I will make a banana juice from this water (pour the water into the glass. It turns yellow).
The second glass becomes woodruff juice (pour the water in and it turns green, repeat twice more).

The third turns into cherry juice (it turns red). The fourth turns into blueberry juice (it turns blue). You see, I conjured up 4 different cocktails from 4 different glasses of water.
That was my magic cocktail bar (take a bow).

Explanation:
Put one drop of food coloring in each of the glasses, before the performance. This you can buy in any grocery store. Use glasses with a thick bottom so that the drops

of color are not seen beforehand. Take them in your hand, covering the bottom of the jar so the color doesn't show.

Tip:
To get the audience involved, ask if anyone knows a magic spell. The children are happy to answer and are especially proud when the trick works with their help. Ask the audience to say the spell together.

Spells

For a magic trick to succeed, cast a spell to go with it.

Well-known spells are:
- Hocus-pocus fidibus,
- Three times black cat
- Sim Sala Bim
- Abracadabra

In one of my performances, a child called out the following spell to me:
"Hocus Pocus Monkey Plunder, watch out a magic miracle."

The audience was visibly amused, which is a plus for any performer.
What actually is a fidibus? Already, Wilhelm Busch mentioned him in his famous work "Max and Moritz," the Fidibus. Very few people know what it actually means. It is even described in the dictionary. The term comes from a time when we all were not yet on earth.
It is a chip of wood or a crumpled strip of paper that was used to light a fire or a pipe.

The rising magic wand

In this trick the magic wand starts to float. You can either perform it alone or in pairs.

Materials:
The made magic wand (about 60 cm long), a thin almost invisible thread, for example fishing line, a 0.33 l transparent bottle, scissors, a paper clip, a table, a thumbtack.

Explanation:
Performer A, the magician, comes on stage. In his hand he holds a bottle, which he places on the table. At the black end of the magic wand is a pin, which is also painted black. The thin invisible magic thread is knotted around the tack.

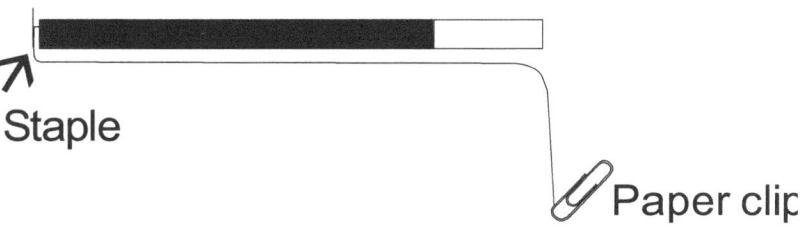

↗
Staple

⬭ Paper clip

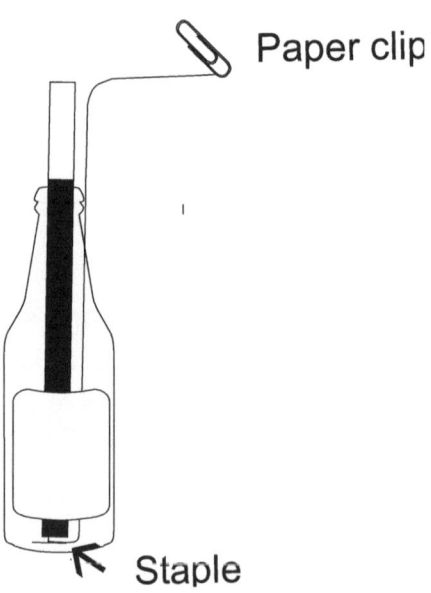

Paper clip

Staple

The paper clip is knotted at the other end of the thread. The black end of the magic wand is in the bottle. The thread rests against the wand and peeks out of the top of the bottle. The paper clip is attached to the magician's pants or belt. Caution. There should be no sweater hanging over it.

Demonstration:
Performer A: I am magician Merlin and I am going to show you a great sensation (he holds his hand at a distance of about 20 cm above the magic wand. The thread is taut. The left foot is one step in front of the right foot. If he rocks slightly backward, the tension of the thread increases and the wand rises in the air. The hand moves up likewise. The spectators would think that there is a connection between the hand and the wand, which could be a thread, for example. If the magician slowly rocks

forward, the tension decreases and the wand sinks back into the bottle. The hand lowers in like manner. The bobbing is not perceptible by the spectators).
You see my rising wand (he repeats the rising a few times).

Actor B: (Has positioned himself half kneeling in some distance and watches the action of his comrade. On the third rising of the wand he intervenes).
(Energetically) Stop! This isn't right. This is pure fraud. I'm going to stop it. (In one hand he visibly holds a pair of scissors. With them, he cuts the apparent connection between hand and wand when the wand is in the air).

Performer A: (Is shocked, Tries to fight him off, but cannot. He moves forward as Performer B cuts, causing the
wand to fall into the bottle from above). What do you
want here? You're disturbing my performance. Don't do
that. Take the scissors away.

(When the supposed thread is cut, he calms down again). And then only real magic will help (he holds his hand over the wand again, snaps the fingers of the other hand and lets the wand rise and fall. He takes the scissors and shows that there are no strings). See. I cut with the scissors and the wand still floats.

Performer B: Oh I can do that too (holds his hand over the wand and guides it up). The wand rises higher and higher and higher (nothing happens).

Performer A: Try it once now (he snaps his fingers).

Performer B: (He tries it and the wand now rises. He lowers it again).

Performer A: In the old days you used an invisible crank to do this (takes an invisible crank from the table, puts it on the bottle and cranks. The rod lifts. He cranks in the other direction and the rod lowers again. He pulls off the crank and puts it back on the table).

Performer B: I can do that too.

Performer A: Try it (gives him the crank).

Performer B: (puts the crank on the bottle. He cranks back and forth, but nothing happens).

Performer A: (Snaps his fingers) now try it again.

Performer B: (Cranks again. Performer A goes back. The wand lifts. Performer A moves forward. Performer B cranks in the other direction and the wand lowers. These movements must be exactly in sync for it to look good).

Performer A: (Pulls off the crank, both bow. The bowing causes the wand to rise once again, which looks quite funny).

The spectators are also amazed, because at the beginning they thought they have seen through the trick. In magic lingo, this is called a "ride-on trick."

If you want to perform this magic trick alone, without a second person, tell the story of the two magicians. Perform all the steps yourself.

The mouse in the cheese house

Materials:
Scissors, glue, a letter clip with a round head, a sheet of photo cardboard, template: mouse and cheese house.

Procedure:
The mouse is put into the cheese house, which the magician closes with a letter clip. It is locked in. The second time it is put in, a spell is cast. Now you can pull out the mouse, although locked.

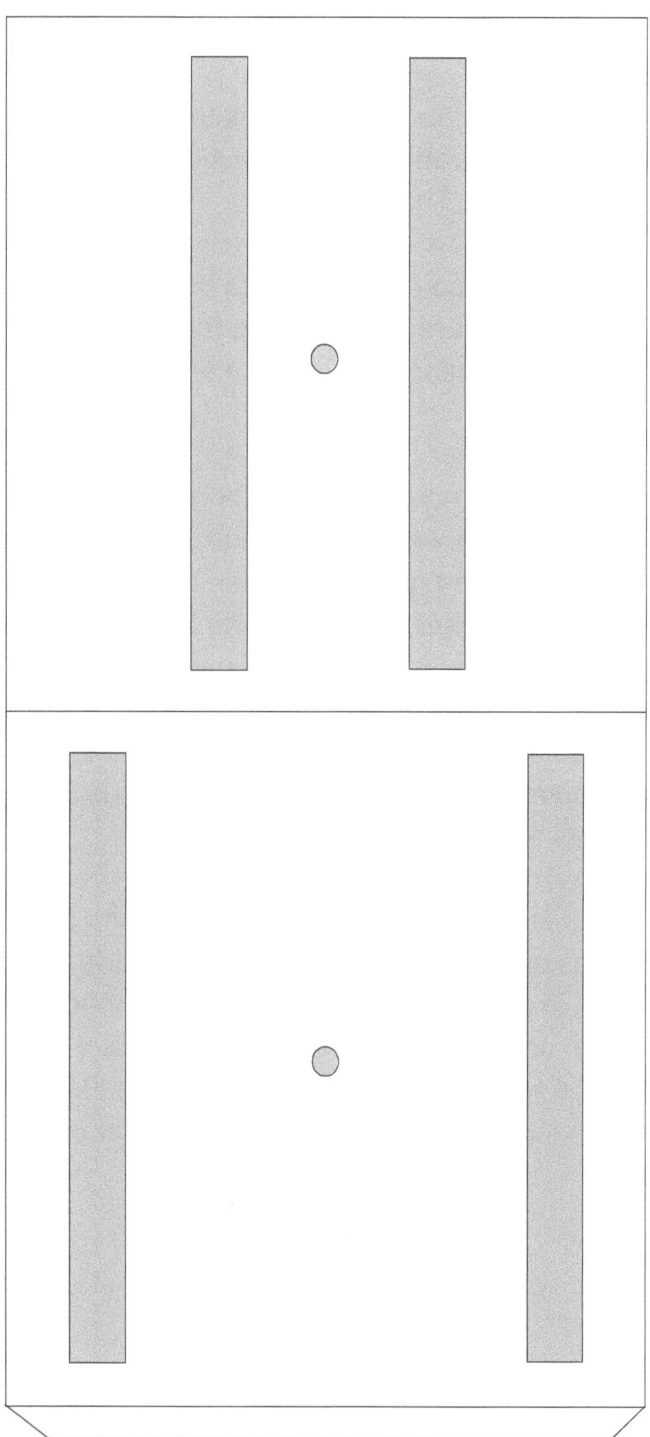

33

Explanation: Cut out the mouse template and glue it on the sheet of photo cardboard to make it more durable and easier to handle. Then color it in.

Glue the cheese house onto the photo board, and cut it out. Cut the hatched areas, as well as the circles in the middle Likewise. Caution: Do not accidentally cut off the glue area.

Now fold the cheese house inward along the center line. The gluing surface as well. Spread glue on the outside of the gluing surface, and glue the cheese house together. This will create a pocket that is open on two sides. The holes in the middle must be on top of each other.

Place the mouse in the cheese house so that the front side of the mouse is sticking out. The front is the side where the slits are farther apart.

The mouse is pushed through the first slot of the front side. It comes out of the first slot of the back side. It is pushed back in through the second slot of the back side, so that it then comes back out on the second slot of the front side. The holes of the mouse and the cheese house are on top of each other so that the letter clip fits through.

Front side (from the audience's point of view)

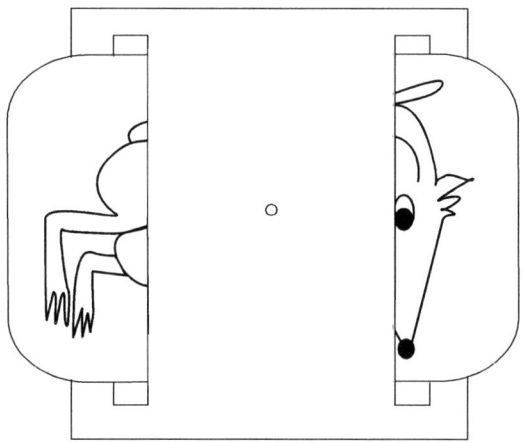

Back side (from the magician's point of view)

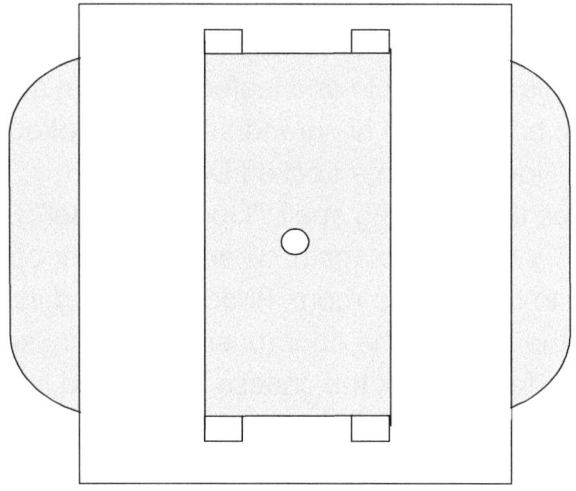

Demonstration:
The magician comes on stage, introduces himself and tells a story.

"Once upon a time there was a mouse named Fridolin. Fridolin lived on a farm (shows the mouse to the audience). There was a cheese room there (shows the cheese room). One day the farmer opened the door to the cheese chamber. Since Fridolin liked to eat cheese so much, he scurried in through the open crack (puts the mouse through the slits into the chamber).

When the farmer left the cheese chamber, he closed the door behind him (inserts letter clip from the front so that the two ends stick out the back and folds over). Fridolin was trapped in the cheese chamber (shakes mouse). Now he had also lost his appetite. It was the next morning that the farmer opened the door again and Fridolin was able to escape (opens the chamber and pulls out the mouse).

"This shall not happen to me again," he said. He went home to his mouse hole and leafed through a magic book that belonged to his grandfather. He looked up the chapter "How to Open a Locked Door."
There was the following spell, "Open Sesame!" He was going to try this. Once again, when the farmer opened the door to the cheese room, Fridolin scurried inside through the crack in the door (pushing the mouse inside). The farmer took the cheese he needed, went outside and locked the door (put the letter clip through the chamber from the back. The head of the clamp is small-

er than the hole of the mouse. This way the staple can slip through and the mouse is free again).

Fridolin ate so much cheese until he could eat no more. When he was full, he stood in front of the door and said "Open sesame!" (Lift the mouse a bit with the thumb, this is not seen by the spectators. Pull the mouse out to the side).
Fridolin was able to disappear through the door, although it was locked (show the cheese chamber)."

Four Ace Trick

Materials:
A deck of 32 cards, a table.

Procedure:
The deck of cards is placed face down on the table. An assistant lifts the deck of cards three times and forms four piles. Now the top cards are dealt from one pile to the other. After that, an ace lies on top of each pile, without the magician having touched the cards and the assistant having lifted off freely at his will.

Explanation:
The deck is prepared so that all 4 aces are face down on top of the deck at the beginning. The deck of cards lies on the stand.

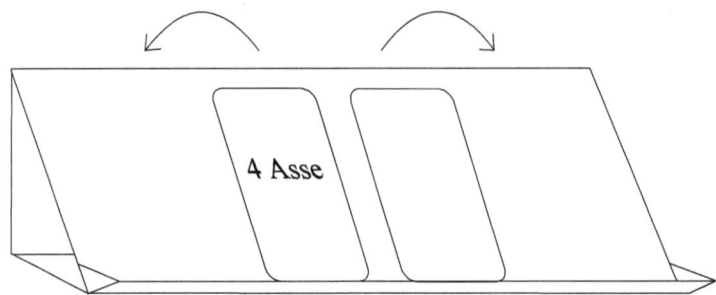

The magician greets the audience, introduces himself and asks one of the spectators to join him. He asks the

assistant to pick up half of the deck of cards and has him place it next to the first pile.
The magician just has to remember which pile contains the four aces.

The assistant is again asked to pick up half of the left pile and place it to the left. Next, from the right pile, making four piles.

The piles 2, 3 and 4 can now be handled as you like. For example, you can put the top 3 cards of the 2nd pile on the 4th pile, then the top 2 cards of the 3rd pile on the 2nd pile.
This game should not be played too long, otherwise the audience will get bored. We come to the essentials.

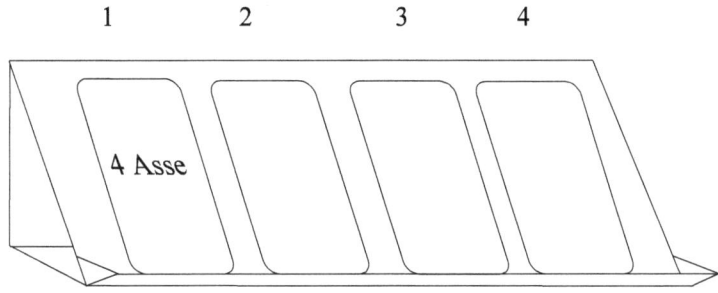

Now you put e.g. 2 cards from the ace pile on the 3rd pile. The assistant can put again e.g. 3 cards from the second pile on the 4th pile. The position of the aces has not changed. 2 are on the first pile and 2 on the third. Now place one card from the 3rd pile on the 2nd pile and one card from the 1st pile on the 4th pile. All 4 aces are now evenly distributed. One ace is now on top of each pile.

This order of lifting is only an example. The magician can, of course, come up with his own order. The only important thing is that he remembers the position of the aces, everything else is pure distraction.

Finally, the assistant should turn over the cards and make sure that there is an ace everywhere. The spectators are allowed to count.

The sword box

We arrive at a highlight. The sword box! It is gladly chosen as the favorite knit of many children.

Materials:
You choose a large box from a TV or a refrigerator.
Width about 60 cm and height about 80 cm, 11 sticks,
paint, brushes.

Procedure:
A child sits down in the magic box. The magician closes
the box. He pushes eleven sticks through the box. Then
he pulls the sticks out again, the child appears, and is
unharmed.

Explanation:
Before the box is painted, the holes for the sticks should
already be in place. The holes are made in the form of a
cube as follows: Five holes each on the left side, and
parallel opposite, five holes on the right side. Five holes
on the back side and five holes on the front side. The
holes on the front and back should be placed a little lower than those on the sides, so that the rods pass each
other. Last but not least, one rod is missing on the top
side.

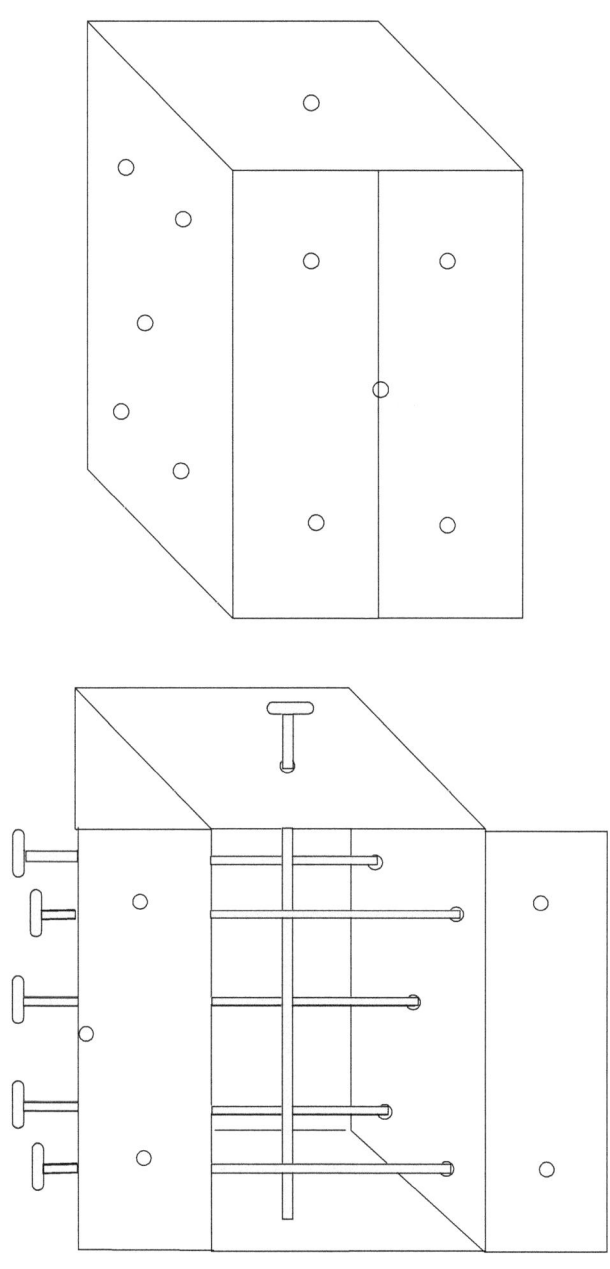

43

The sticks can be made from old field hockey sticks, for example, or from broomsticks painted silver. They should be at least 1 m long so that they stick out about 20 cm on both sides of the crate.

Now you can paint the crate. It is best to use finger paints for this. Put newspaper under the crate so that no paint drips on the floor.

Demonstration:

The sword box stands on the end on the stage with the opening facing the audience. The front flaps serve as doors and are closed. Next to it is an old washing drum, nicely painted or pasted, in which the sticks, excuse me, the swords are placed. This trick is most effectively performed with atmospheric music, which increases the tension immensely.

Two children are needed as performers. One child plays the magician, while the other one plays the assistant who gets into the box and is pierced.

The magician comes on stage, followed by his assistant. He introduces his assistant and then himself. He briefly explains that his assistant will climb into the box. Next, the music is turned on. Excitedly, the swords are pushed into the box, one by one. The magician slides them in first from the front so that the doors remain closed, then from the side, and finally from the top.

The assistant inside the crate helps to make sure that the swords on the opposite holes are pushed back out. There is enough space for the assistant inside the crate to sit between the bars. At most, he has to contort a bit and sit at an angle when the middle bars are pushed through. From the audience's point of view, however, it looks much more dramatic. It looks as if the person is actually being pierced. To make sure the audience is convinced that all the swords have pierced through, the box is rotated around itself once. The music is turned down so the magician can say, "So that you can see that my assistant (name) is still in the box, he will stick his hand out and wave a cloth at you." The assistant obeys this.

Now the rods are pulled out one by one again in reverse order.
First the top one, then the ones from the side, and finally the ones in front. During the thunderous applause, the assistant jumps out of the box and presents himself, spreading both arms. Everyone takes a bow.

Giant bubbles

Between the magic interludes, soap bubbles provide a welcome change. They stimulate the imagination and entice people to dream.
Included in the magic performance, they elicit "AHs" and OHs" from the audience, who are happy to be amazed.
In this case, they are even giant soap bubbles.
They became famous thanks to the clown Pic, who performed a giant soap bubble act in the Roncalli Circus.

There are many gimmicks with soap bubbles. It is worth trying them out, turning small bubbles into big ones, letting them float or bouncing a giant soap bubble on the created membrane on the previously dipped bubble ring.

Just performing the giant soap bubbles as a number in the performance to atmospheric music puts the audience in an enthusiastic mood.

Meanwhile, there are many ready-made mixtures to buy. But there is also the possibility of making the liquid and the utensils yourself. You need a bubble ring, liquid and of course a container.

The bubble ring

Materials:
Bucket, a bamboo stick (you can get it in any building and garden market or craft store), diameter 1 cm, length 1 m, floral wire, and thick wire.

This bubble ring is big enough to be performed with on stage in front of several people. It is easily visible to the audience. It doesn't need to be blown through with this size ring like the small ones. You can simply move it through the air, for example from left to right. You will see how a bulge is created and how a huge soap bubble is formed. If it gets too big, it will easily burst before it is completed. With a little practice you can estimate the size so that it does not burst, but flies as a ball billowing through the air. A little trick is to turn the bubble ring to close the bubble.

1. You need about 61 cm of the thick wire. Clip it off with a pair of pliers.
2. From the thick wire, bend a circle about 18 cm in diameter. Leave 3 cm at each end. Bend the ends down and place them on the bamboo stick.
3. Using floral wire, attach the circle to the wire.
4. Using two floral wires, wrap them, ensuring the floral wires are in opposite directions, around the thick wire. This will create a loop-like structure. Wrap the ends around the stick, and pinch them off with pliers. Make

sure they are well hidden so no one can hurt themselves.
5. When this ring is immersed in the liquid, it will stick as a surface (membrane).

Recipe:
- 3 ½ l of water
- 375 ml of neutral soap
- 250 g of sugar
- 20 g of paste powder

Please prepare the mixture one day in advance. It is important to stir it several times.
If you need a larger amount than indicated here, just double the amount of ingredients.
Have fun trying it out!

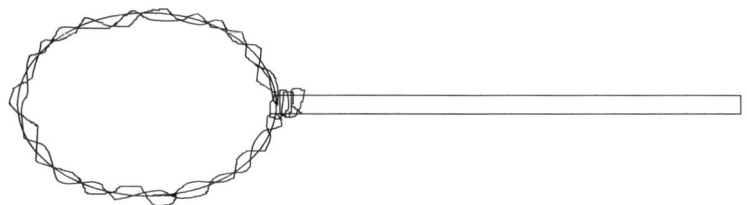

Do you also love the iridescent colors of the soap bubbles that float silently down? Take a bucket big enough for enough liquid to fit the ring easily.

You can also get a bucket with a lid. Snack bars use them for mayonnaise or yogurt sauce. They often get thrown away.

If you have a lid, the liquid won't evaporate as quickly. Another option is to bottle the liquid after each sample.

Cover the outside with colorful foil and magic items. This way, the bucket will also play its part to in demonstration.

Please put paper or a plastic sheet under it in the rehearsal and in the performance, because the burst bubbles are very slippery on the floor.

If it's especially cold outside, you can also blow frozen bubbles. This looks especially graceful.

The broken match

The spectator assistant puts a marked match in a cloth. It is then folded. The assistant breaks the match. The magician conjures it whole again.

Materials:
Tea towel or large cloth handkerchief with a wide hem, matches, needle and thread, pencil for marking, and table.

Explanation:
A match is pushed into the hem of the cloth before the demonstration. If the hem is not big enough, you can fold the edge a little and sew it tight so that a match fits inside. The match is not visible from the outside. The magician feels where the match is though.

Demonstration:
The cloth lies on a table. Observe in which corner the match is located.
After getting an assistant on stage, tell the assistant to take a match out of the box and mark it with a pen. Spread the cloth on the table. The assistant places the marked match in the center of the cloth. Take the corners of the cloth one by one and cover them over the match, starting with the corner where the prepared match is in the hem.
A small packet is formed. Observe in which position the prepared match is. It should be right next to the other one.

Take the match and give it to the assistant who will break it. Please keep it close above the table so that the other match does not accidentally slip out.

Put the cloth back on the table. Make a magical motion above the cloth with the wand, carefully grab the tip and slowly lift it up. The marked match falls on the table. The wizard witnesses that it is his match and you get your well-deserved applause.

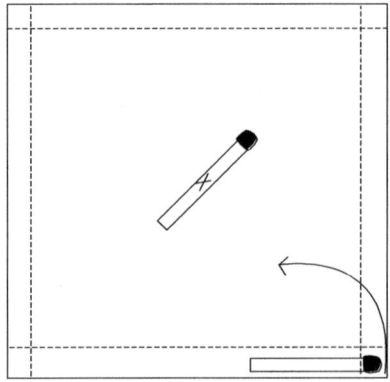

Tip: If you do pick the wrong match, it's not so bad. It may well increase the tension. Repeat the procedure, blaming everything on the fact that there is still a spell to be cast, and then let the right match break.

Fish market trick

Materials:
Tissue paper, glue, scissors, salt shaker, and pencil.

Procedure :
A strip of tissue paper is torn into several pieces and
magically made whole again with the help of magic salt.

Explanation:
Of course, the magician needs 2 identical strips, which
he secretly mixes up. The strips are 56 cm long and 6
cm wide. One strip is prepared as follows: At one end,
glue a small pocket into which the second strip will fit.
Fold about 10 cm from the beginning of the strip, glue it
and the flap is created. It must be big enough for the
second strip to fit in and not slip out.

On the remaining strip is the following saying:
"Today here sale of fresh fish."
Please do not start writing until after the pocket act.
Write the same saying on the second strip. This strip is
folded in an accordion shape and pushed into the pock-
et. The folds should be about 2 cm apart.

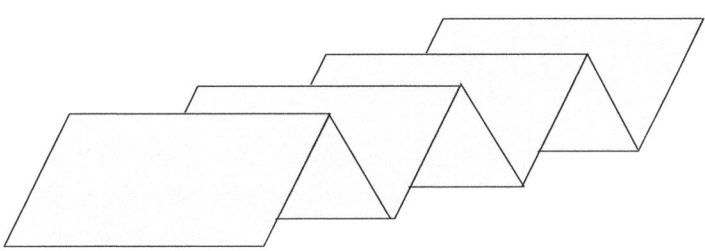

Demonstration:
Place the salt shaker in your pants pocket. Hide (palm) the pocket in your right hand. The fingers are in front of the bag as seen from the audience. The back of the hand is turned toward the audience. The left hand is held in the same position, except that it is just not hiding anything, just holding the end.

Today here sale of fresh fish

Narrate: The other day I was in Hamburg at the fish market. I was strolling through the market and spotted a stall with the following sign on it:
"Today here sale of fresh fish."

I thought, that's a long sign. Surely it is clear that the fish are sold today and not yesterday or tomorrow. So "to-day" is redundant. I went to the sign, took it in my hand and tore it off.
(First, the bag is torn off. It is placed in front of the strip, behind the word "today" so the audience can still read

the strip, then "today" is torn off. The bag and "today" is put in front of the strip).

Now it still reads "here sale of fresh fish". It's only logical, I thought, that the fish are sold here and not over there, it's just as superfluous and is torn down ("here" is torn down. The whole heap is put behind the strip, so that the bag is facing the wizard).
"Sale of fresh fish." "Sale" is really superfluous, so it can go ("sale" is torn down).
"of fresh fish." That's no way to start a sentence ("of" is torn down).
"I mean, everyone knows that the fish are fresh ("fresh" is torn off).
Fish", everyone can see that they are fish and not elephants or ants, right?

Now there was no sign there. Suddenly the saleswoman came. When she saw what I had done to her sign, she got very angry. She scolded. "What are you doing? You can't tear up my whole sign. Now no one can see from afar that there is a booth here." The good woman was right. And how fortunate that I am a sorceress and always have magic salt with me.
(At this time, the bag lying on top of the pile is torn open with the index finger. The strips are folded left and right around the pile. Two separate piles are formed. The second prepared strip is replaced unnoticed. The snippets are transported unnoticed into the trouser pocket.

It goes like this:

The entire pile is placed in the palm of the right hand. The two piles are separated by the thumb pushing the pile of the folded strip between the thumb and index finger. The snippets that are not visible from the audience remain palmed in the palm of the hand.

The left hand takes over the folded strip, visibly held by the thumb and index finger. The left hand moves forward away from the body and presents it to the audience. The right hand reaches into the pocket of the pants, leaves the paper scraps there and takes out the magic salt with it. Sprinkle the magic salt over the strip, unfold it and hold it out for the audience to read).

So I conjured the sign whole again and the saleswoman smiled with satisfaction (bow and show that the hands are empty).

The hypnosis number

Material:
2 broomsticks, 1 pair of old shoes, old jeans pants, 1 pair of old stockings, fabric for a cape, and 1 chair.

Procedure: The magician hypnotizes his assistant and makes her levitate.

Explanation:
The assistant holds two fake legs, which she clamps under her arm. The legs are built as follows:
Cloth is wrapped around the lower part of the broomsticks to make them as thick as legs. The wrapped end of the stiles stick into the shoes, whose laces are tied around the stiles. If they do not hold, you can additionally pin them to the stem. From a pair of pants cut off the trouser legs, about 50 cm.

Attach the trouser legs to the stems with, for example, masking tape. The end of the trouser leg protrudes slightly above the shoe. This creates the perfect mockup of two dressed legs.
The stems are held under the arms, as in stilt walking, so that they can be easily lifted. The assistant bends the arms at this. The poles lie below the armpits along the body and end behind the shoulder. The hands point down with the thumbs and grip the stilt.

The robe:
It consists of two old sheets. They are superimposed and sewn together at the A and B sides. At the corner A/B (see arrow), 25 cm each remain open, through which the head is to be put.
The assistant puts her head back and lifts the two fake legs horizontally upwards. The illusion is created as if she is floating. To facilitate this, there should be a chair at the foot end, on the back of which the assistant can place the false feet.

Demonstration:
The magician introduces himself as Sheik El Achmed, who comes from a distant land. He asks his assistant to come on the stage (she trifles in. In fact, she has to pass off the fake legs as her real feet. She apparently walks with the wrong feet. She copies her own gait. She lifts her feet and puts one in front of the other. Synchronous-ly, she moves her real feet, but no one is allowed to see them. She and the magician make sure that the robe always stays on the floor and only the front the fake feet peek out).

A

B

He greets his assistant Princess Suleika and explains to the audience that he wants to hypnotize her (by all the rules of the art, he hypnotizes her).

"Look me in the eyes, listen to my words and obey what I tell you. You are getting tired, more and more tired. Your eyelids are getting heavier and heavier. Your eyes are falling shut. You begin to sleep. Imagine your body becoming light, lighter and lighter, as light as a feather. You become lighter and lighter. Nothing can hold you to the ground and you start to lift yourself into the air, very slowly. You begin to float, higher and higher, until your whole body is floating."

(When the legs lift, care must be taken to keep the robe on the floor. If it lifts, the real feet can be seen and the trick has failed. When the assistant floats, the magician presents himself and receives his applause. After that, he makes her get heavier again).

"You get heavier and heavier again. The feather turns to lead and you float towards the ground again until your feet touch the ground. I count slowly to three and when I clap my hands, you wake up again. One, two, three (claps hands and assistant opens eyes. Both bow)."

The number works especially well when quiet, calm sphere music is playing in the background and the magician speaks his hypnosis in a monotonous singsong. This creates the right effect while floating.

The rabbit in the top hat

With this trick you can show your friends how to make a rabbit out of a hat. You can find the rabbit on the next page.

Instructions:
You will need a hat, a dark or black cloth about 45 cm x 45 cm, photo cardboard, a thread in the color of the hat, a needle, a cardboard bunny and a paper clip.

Create the bunny as follows:
- Copy the bunny template
- Cut it out
- Glue it on the cardboard
- Cut out the cardboard, this way you will get Schnuffi the magic bunny.

Preparation:
- Get a dark cloth. Tie the paper clip to one end of the thread. Attach the other end to the edge of the cloth in the middle.
If you have a cylinder, use it. Otherwise, you can use any other hat.
- Attach the bunny to the paper clip. The thread is 2/3 of the length of the ink so that the bunny hangs in the cloth and is not visible. It should not peek out at the bottom.

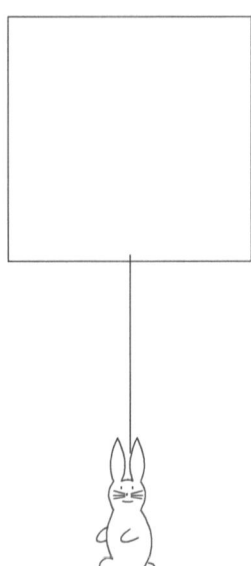

Demonstration: Place the hat in front of you on the table. Put the crumpled cloth next to it. The rabbit is inside the cloth.
- Show your audience that the hat is empty.
- Take the cloth and hold it up by the edge where the thread is hanging.
 The rabbit is now hanging on the inside of the cloth by the thread. It cannot be seen.
- Let the rabbit hang inside the hat.
 You can show the cloth empty from both sides.
- Cover the hat with the cloth.
- Cast a spell and make a magic movement with the wand.
- Take off the cloth and put it on the side of the hat facing away from the audience. The rabbit and the thread will not be noticed.
- Reach into the hat and show the rabbit. Remove the paper clip.

2. Accessories for conjuring

Making the magic wand

The most important prop for the magician is the magic wand. It supports the magical atmosphere or serves as a distraction from the actual trick. It is used in every performance.

But please do not point it at living people. Something can easily happen and you turn someone into a frog and then don't know the spell to turn them back. So, be careful with it.

Materials:
1 round stick (diameter 1 cm and length 30 cm) 1 brush, black and white plaka or varnish paint, and saw.

Making the magic wand is quite simple. The round stick, which is made of wood, is sold by the meter and you can get it in any craft store. Saw it to the right length.

1. Mark the rod after 30 cm. Clamp the rod in a vice. If you don't have one, take two chairs and place the rod between them. Let the ends hold. Now saw the rod to the right length.
3. If the ends are rough, file them smooth with some sandpaper.
4. Next, paint the stick. To do this, lay newspaper or paper from the wastepaper roll on the table.

The wand comes in several variations. We prefer to paint one end about 5 cm white and the rest black.

The magic box

Some magic utensils accumulate and need a place to be put.
A homemade magic box is ideal. I have used shoe boxes in my courses, which proved to be very valuable thanks to their stability. A matching lid comes with it.
Ask in a shoe store for empty shoe boxes with lids. You have made a contribution by not allowing valuable material to be thrown into the garbage. This is also called "sustainability".

You can paint your box with bright colors, using for example, finger paints, which can also be applied with a brush. Paint the box with magic symbols.

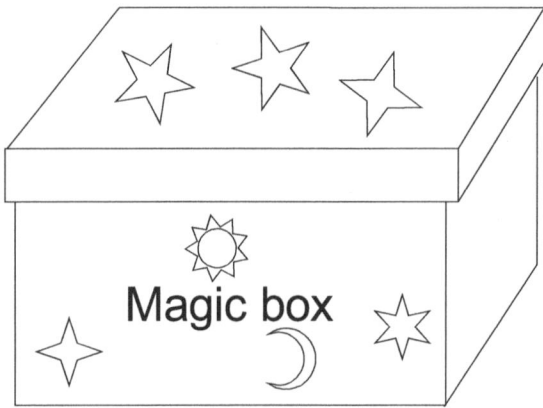

This activity is a lot of fun and encourages creative work. In the box, you can collect the magic tricks that were made. In this way, you have ensured that order is created in a playful way, and that the tricks are not scattered around the room.

Magic Symbols

The most important magic symbols are the pentagram, also called the five-pointed star, and the crescent moon. Here is a sample so you'll be able to draw them neatly.

The Crescent Moon
Take a round glass. Place it upside down on the sheet of paper. Draw the outline halfway with a pencil. A half circle is created. Pull the glass a little to the side. Draw the edge of the glass again and connect it with the first half circle. The result is a half moon.

The Pentagram
How do I draw a regular five-pointed star with one stroke? This is very simple! Start drawing in the lower left corner. Draw a line diagonally upwards to the right. (1). Next, draw a horizontal line to the left (2). Then draw a line down to the right (3). From there up to the center (4). And finally connect it to the beginning in the lower left corner (5).

Perfect! Congratulations. If you can remember this, you will draw the best stars.

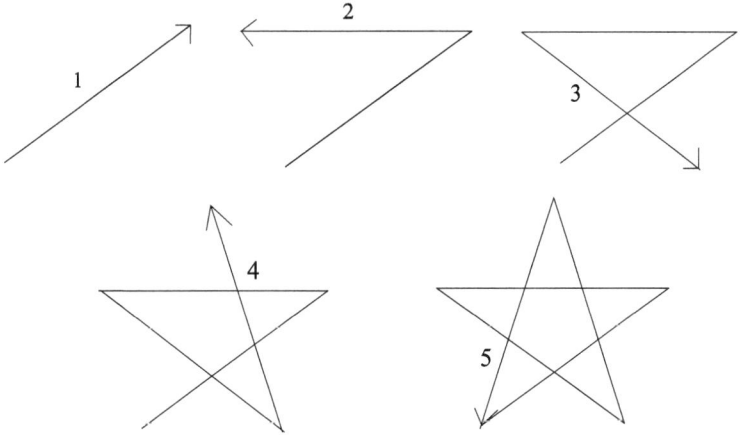

The magic hat

Material:
A sheet of photo cardboard, scissors, glue, gold foil, pencil, string, hat elastic, and possibly a tucker or clothespins.

To make the performance more magical, a magic hat should not be missing. Get some colorful photo card-stock. You can get it at any craft store. It is available in the size 50 x 70 cm.

1. To make a hat out of the sheet, cut out a quarter circle that is 50 cm long on both sides. You can choose to draw the quarter circle with a compass. If you don't have a compass at hand, make one yourself.

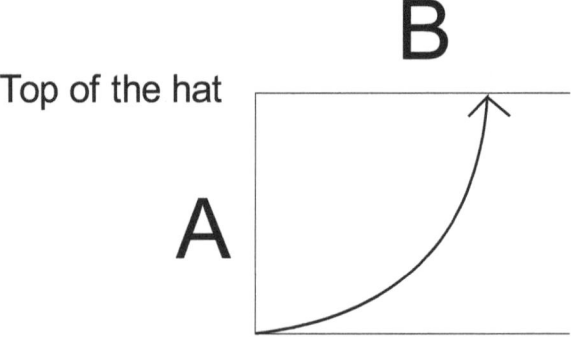

Top of the hat

2. Take a pencil and attach a piece of string that is as long as the long end of the bow to the bottom. If you hold the pencil to the bottom corner of the bow and the other

end of the string to the top corner, you can draw an exact quarter circle.

3. Cut out the circle section.

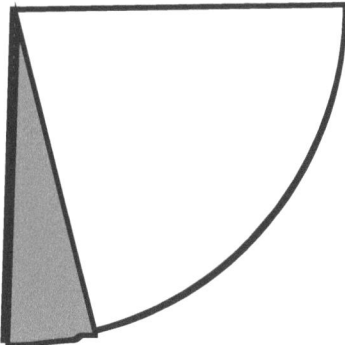

4. Holding the sides A and B on top of each other, you can measure the head size on your head and adjust the hat exactly. Mark the spot. Draw a line from the mark to the top. Use this area as a glue line.
A pointed hat will be created.
Hold the hat together with a clothespin until it dries so it doesn't gap again.

5. Drill a hole in the cardboard on each of the two sides, pull a hat elastic through it and knot it so the hat won't slip off your head later on.
6. Glue the hat to your taste with gold foil, stars, moons or magical things.

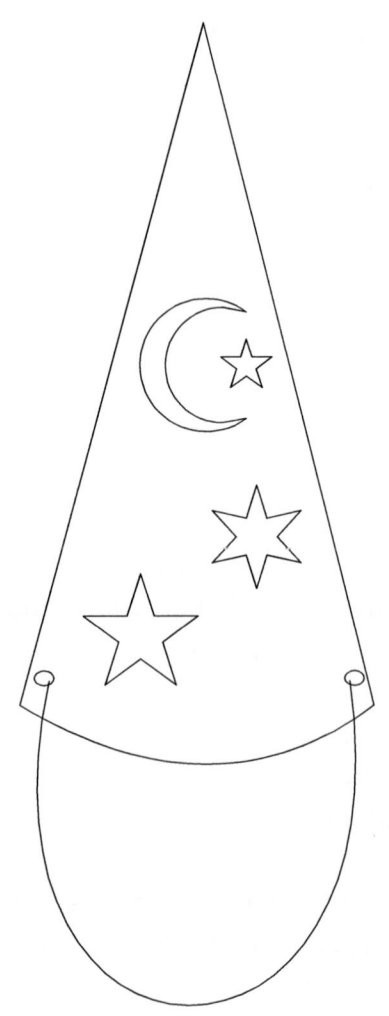

To add a brim to the hat, do the following:

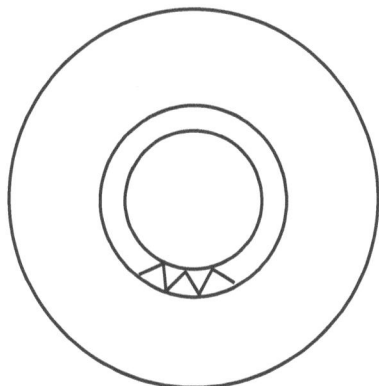

1. Before you attach the hat elastic, place the hat on another piece of photo card and trace the brim.
2. Draw another circle at a distance of 15 cm. This is the outer brim of the hat.
3. Inside the circle, draw a smaller circle 2 cm apart.
4. Draw 2 cm wide prongs inside the entire narrow circle, pointing to the center of the circle. They will serve as a gluing surface. Cut out the prongs all around and fold them up.
Put glue on the front side of the prongs and glue the hat on top so that the prongs are stuck inside the hat. Now it is a real magic hat.
Attach the rubber band to the hat as described above.
Drill 2 small holes 2 cm apart on each side of the hat and knot the rubber.

3. Preparation for the performance

The presentation on stage

The presentation of what you have learned, as well as yourself on stage is just as important as practicing the tricks. The magician is a role that is being played. Everyone who is a magician slips into this role and is therefore an actor. The stage is his field of action. It acts as a magnifying glass through which even the smallest movement is perceived.

Therefore, there are important points that you should pay attention to and that can be practiced during the rehearsal.

1 - Come on stage smiling

After all, the audience should see that the performer enjoys performing magic. Often, performers are plagued by stage fright and are very excited. Stage fright before the performance is part of it. Even if it seems unbearable, this reaction of the body increases our ability to concentrate. Any actor will say the same. Once the performance has begun, everything goes by frantically. When the performance is over, we can really enjoy the applause and the success.

Smiling is friendly and arouses sympathy in the audience. So appear radiant on stage, unless the role dictates playing a different character. This applies to the

whole time you are on stage. Smiling also psychological-
ly helps you stay loose and not tensed up.

2 - Speak loudly and clearly

It's dangerous for any performer if the audience doesn't
understand anything. First, someone asks their neighbor
what the magician said and then the next person, until it
propagates to the last row. It creates a commotion that
even a professional has trouble stopping. That's why the
number one motto for each performer is to speak loudly
and clearly so that even the audience in the back row
understands everything.

3 - Introduce yourself at the beginning

It is often difficult to find a starting point, especially when
you are alone on stage. Therefore, a good way to start is
to first greet the audience and then introduce yourself.
This is done as an introduction to the event, so to speak,
so that the audience knows who is in front of them. Pick
a stage name for this. It immediately establishes a personal connection between performer and audience.
Famous names for magicians include David Copperfield,
the Ehrlich Brothers, Kalanag, Siegfried and Roy, etc.

4 - Never stand with your back to the audience

It's not just rude to turn your back to the audience. In the
first place, the audience does not see what is going on.

Moreover, they do not hear what is being said. Inattention, from which in turn restlessness arises, is the result. Therefore, it is important to be face to face with the audience so that the connection is not broken. Exceptions are again when the role dictates otherwise.

5 - Looking at the audience while talking and playing.

The connection created and the attention it brings between performer and audience are maintained when the performer looks at and addresses them. It is not advisable to stare only at one point in the audience or only at the front row audience. The gaze should move from one spectator to another so that everyone feels addressed and the magician can survey everything. If the lighting conditions do not allow you to recognize every spectator because of too glaring spotlights, the sight is nevertheless indicated in a visionary way. But this should not be done with narrowed eyes.

Any spectator who has the feeling that he is being looked at directly by the performer will now be inattentive and turn away from what is happening on stage.

6 - Never anticipate the result

I have already explained this in connection with the cloth trick. Never predict the outcome. If I say "I'm going to show you how I'm going to turn the cloth into a ball," the audience will look for the hiding place of the ball. They are no longer surprised when this actually happens because they already knew.

7 - Don't let on when something goes wrong

Anyone can go wrong once in a while, even the professionals. It doesn't matter. However, it's important not to let on. Don't start swearing. Stay loose, just keep playing if you can. "Improvisation is everything," as the saying goes.

The audience doesn't know what's going to happen. They don't know the sequence of events. Most of the time, the audience thinks it's planned and that it's part of the performance.

8 - Bow at the end

To give the audience a sign that the performance is over, a bow is just ideal. The audience starts applauding at the latest when the bow is taken. It is a tribute and thanksgiving to the audience for listening and applauding for so long.

9 - Do not speak while applauding.

This is one of the biggest mistakes that is made over and over again. When the audience applauds, for example, during an interlude or scene applause during the performance, the magician should in no case continue speaking. He can take a short break and wait until the applause is over. Only then can he continue speaking.

Otherwise, the audience might miss important details. They are grateful for it, satisfied and able to concentrate on the sequence of events that follows.

The interactions between performer and audience are important. The audience must be convinced that a miracle is really happening on stage that they cannot explain.

Assistants on stage

An important factor in the performance are assistants from the audience. They bring diversity to the action and are often the reason for an interlude of applause.

Keep in mind that assistants are not used to being on stage in front of an audience. If the magician says "And now I need an assistant", children should not be volunteers. If someone is found, he should be asked to come. If no one can be found, someone who seems appropriate is chosen and asked to come.

Make sure that he or she does not have his or her back to the audience. If this is the case, you politely ask him to turn around, shake his hand and ask his name. He is introduced and the performer asks for a big round of applause, which is gladly given by the audience.

The assistant should always be the winner. The tasks given to him should be easy to perform so that he remains relaxed and is not afraid. If the assistant is still very young, his disposition often provides small laughs and increases the attention of the audience. You just have to make sure that he also understands the flow of the trick. He should be treated politely to take away his fear and to show future assistants that it is fun to be on stage.

One suggestion is to give the assistant a reward for helping, such as a chocolate magic thaler.
No joke should go off at the expense of the assistants, otherwise they would certainly have been assistants for the last time.

When practicing tricks, dealing with assistants is definitely part of the process. When the trick is over and he has completed his task, you thank him, ask him to take his seat again, and of course he receives another big round of applause. After that, the magician takes a bow and continues in the program.

Select music

Some numbers can be performed without speaking. Speech would only be distracting and not create the right mood. For these numbers, the appropriate background music is very important.

It enhances and emphasizes the mood of the performance, and creates feelings. Through music, our emotions can be sad, elated, excited, or we are transported to mystical regions. Television knows only too well the effect of music, which it deliberately uses in all films.

But there are other situations during the show where music is appropriate in the background. It serves to bridge the time between the individual scenes.

At the beginning, when the audience enters the auditorium and takes its seats, there is a tension of expectation until the performance begins. We all experience this when we go to the theater.

In order to get the audience in the right mood for the upcoming performance, music befitting the number is appropriate. One possibility for our magic performance is circus music, which of course must fit the performance.

Suitable music is:

Queen - It's a kind of magic
Queen - We are the champions
Vangelis - Conquest of paradise
Vangelis - Chariots of fire
Europe - It's a final countdown
Wayne - Eve of the war
Axel. F. - Faltermeyer
Charlie Chaplin - Limelight
Michael Jackson - Heal the world
Tina Turner - The best
Andreas Vollenweider - Caverna magica
Art of noise - Moments in love

Set the order of the tricks

Once all the tricks are practiced and crafted, set the order of the tricks. Start with a simple trick. Finally, end with a climax. Progress in such a manner that the difficulty of the performances increases during the show and the tension curve rises.

The music and speech numbers should be performed alternately. In the same way, it is advisable that tricks with and without assistants alternate.
Since the spectators are still a little uncertain at the beginning, do not start with a trick for which you need an assistant from the first audience. This should only be considered from the second trick on.

Variety is the first rule. Excitement should alternate with relaxation.

Greeting the spectators

A greeting announcement could look like this:
"Good afternoon my dear audience. I would like to welcome you to my magic show. I am very pleased that so many of you have made out time to come.

Please raise your right arm once. Raise it horizontally in front of your body (you do all the movements). The audience joins in the exercise. Wait until everyone has their arm extended), and then raise your left arm to the same height.

Slowly bring the hands together until they meet (a clapping sound is made). Again apart and again together, and faster and faster until applause is formed (here the audience is encouraged to join in for the first time).

A nice sound is created. Next, go like, "and whenever you like something, please let me hear that sound (the audience escapes its stiff atmosphere and becomes relaxed and attuned to applause from the beginning)."

4. Twisting balloons

Figures from twisting balloons

Balloons, with their bright colors, offer a special charm for a magic show. An unusual type of balloons are modeling balloons. They can be kneaded, squeezed, pressed, twisted and all kinds of crazy figures, animals or objects can be formed from them. Watching this is very exciting for the spectators.

Marvin Hardy, a well-known balloon modeler, makes the most fascinating figures with them. There is virtually nothing he cannot model. He even modeled a dress that was worn at a fashion show.

Balloons are also a great way to give a small gift and say thank you to an assistant for his/her help.
You can include them in a magic show, make them appear, or have them perform a trick themselves.

You can buy the balloons in balloon stores, toy stores, juggling stores or magic stores.
Since they are difficult to blow up by mouth and there are chemicals in the balloons to keep them from sticking, it is advisable to use a balloon pump (with a pointed opening). These pumps have a double action pumping force. They blow air into the balloon while pulling and pushing the pump piston.

In commerce there are different shapes of balloons, thick, thin, long and short. The most popular size is 260, which is about 140 cm long when inflated and has a diameter of about 4 cm. It is best to get about 100 of it so that they are enough for practicing and for the performance.

Waterproof pens in all colors are suitable for painting the balloons. Black is almost always good.

Max, the balloon dog

How do you sculpt a dog out of a long, thin balloon? Here you can find the instructions.

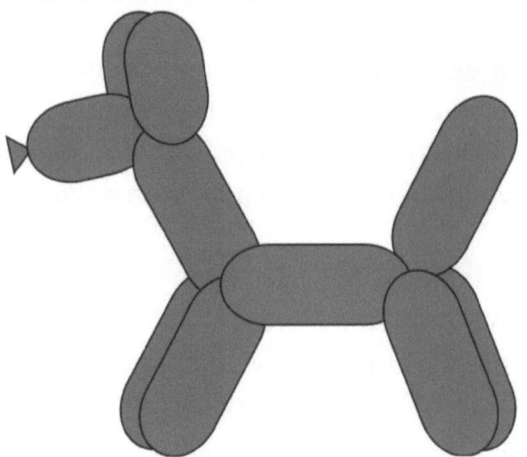

Materials: Modeling balloon and balloon pump.

First, pull the balloon lengthwise to stretch it.

Do not inflate it fully. Leave about 12 cm uninflated. If you have inflated too much, you can let the air out again. When modeling the individual balloon bubbles (bubbles), air is always pushed to the back, which needs space.

If there is nothing left, the balloon would be too thick and would burst. Knot the balloon. Always start kneading at the front of the knot.

Instructions:
First, make 3 balloon bubbles. Pull the balloon a few times to stretch it before inflating.
Put the pump on the mouthpiece and inflate the balloon, leaving a small tip. Let out some air again so that a tip of 6 cm remains uninflated.

After 8 cm from the mouthpiece, press the balloon in with your thumb and index finger, and turn the resulting bubble around itself three times.

Hold the first bubble with your hand, and after 8 cm twist another bubble in the same direction.

Now fold the balloon over so that the bubble is next to the second one. This way you can hold bubble 1 and 2 loosely.

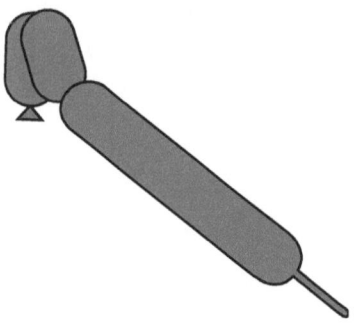

Twist off another 8 cm bubble. Press the first and second indentation together and twist bubbles 2 and 3 together several times. When you let go, the 3 bubbles are fixed.

You have formed the head. A nose with two ears.

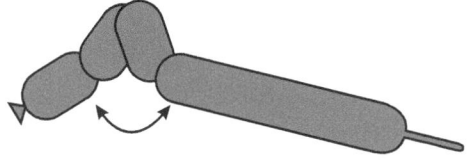

Take the balloon in your left hand. After 8 cm, twist off a bubble that forms the neck. Continue to hold the bubble.

For the front legs, create 2 more bubbles, each 8 cm long, and twist them together, the same way you formed the head.

Fold the second front leg next to the first and twist them at the indentation. This way they are fixed.

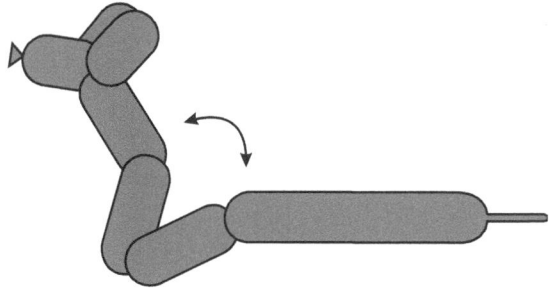

For the belly, twist off a 15 cm long bubble. Hold it tight so it doesn't untwist.

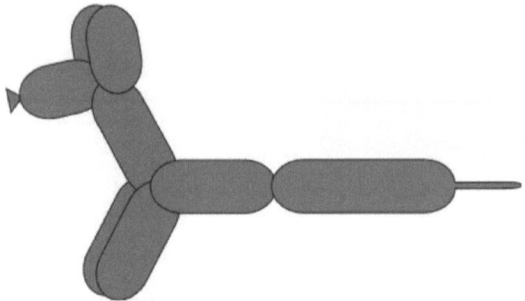

If the balloon is too bulging, press on the bubble and push some air towards the uninflated tip.

Now it's the turn of the back legs. Create 2 bubbles, each having a length of 8 cm. Twist them like the front legs.

The rest of the balloon makes the tail. If there is a small uninflated nipple that bothers you, push some air from the tail into it. Take the tail in both hands and push the air up.

The dog is ready!

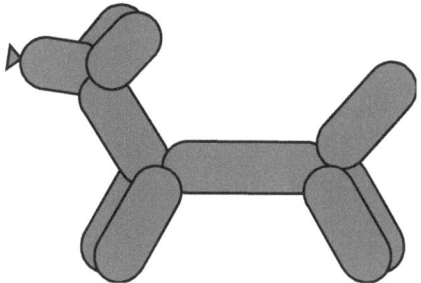

If you feel like it, you can now paint the balloon with a waterproof pen. Paint its eyes, whiskers and anything else you can think of.

A mouse

Leave 2/3 of the balloon uninflated. If you make the bubbles only a few inches tall, the figure described above will be smaller. Then you have made a mouse.

A giraffe

You can easily create a giraffe. Leave 8 cm uninflated. Model the neck bubble of the dog figure longer.

A poodle

For the poodle, you need some space at the end of the balloon, because a small round balloon should appear there. Leave about 15 cm of the balloon uninflated. Make the body smaller. Make a 6-7 cm bubble.

Put the long piece on the dog's tail in the mouth. Suck on it and at the same time push the air from the tail up with your fingers. A small round bubble will appear at the end. This is the trademark of a poodle.
Magic with the poodle
Go over the bubble at the tail end of the poodle with your right hand.
Take the bubble in your fist. Push the air back into the tail. Gesture as if you are pulling this bubble off with your hand and blow the invisible ball into the air. It is conjured away.
Conjure it up again by repeating the procedure in reverse. Reach into the air and hold an invisible bubble. Put it in your mouth. Put the tip of the tail in your mouth and suck on it.
It's back on the balloon dog's tail.

Animation with the poodle

1. Clamp the dog under your right arm so that you can grasp the neck with your right hand.
2. Say that Max is a very bright dog. Turn the neck back and forth so that the head looks in several directions.
3. Take out invisible food from your pants or jacket pocket with your left hand and hold it in front of his muzzle.

4. Move the snout into your hand and make a few eating movements. This is how Max the balloon dog comes to life.
5. Hold the dog with your left hand and take its tail between your right thumb and index finger. Move the tail back and forth.
6. Explain that this is a sign of joy if he liked it.
7. Max listens to your word. Only you must not say "Make way", otherwise he will burst.

This animation is especially fun for younger children.

Max the card magician

But Max, the balloon poodle, can do even more. He can even do magic. His favorite magic is with cards. However, this requires some dexterity and is therefore more suitable for older children.

Materials:
1 balloon dog, deck of cards with box, and a table.

Actors
One magician and one assistant from the audience.

Effect
The assistant draws a card from the deck and returns it. The deck is put into the box and closed. Max, the balloon dog, pulls out the spectator's card from the box.

Explantation

Part 1: The preparation of the deck of cards
1. Take the deck of cards out of the box and fan it apart.
The assistant may pull out any card. He looks at it and
shows it to the audience.
2. The fan is pushed together. The deck of cards is in
your left palm. Your thumb is on the left side of the deck,
your index finger is on top, and the rest of your fingers
are on the right side of the deck.
3. Keep a gap in the middle by sliding your thumb between the cards. Hold the top half with your right hand,
place the index finger on the left and the thumb on the
bottom of the stack. The assistant slides his card into
this gap.
4. The box is next to you on the table. The assistant
stands on the other side. Turn to face the box. While
turning, pull off the top pile and slide it under the deck of
cards. This is done very quickly, so it is not noticeable.
Practice well!

The drawn card is now on top of the deck.
The box has a flap at the top and a notch in the front to
make it easier to slide the flap in.
Slide the pile into the box so that the picture side faces
the back of the box and the drawn card is at the notch.
Slide the tab in behind the first card so that it is between
the first and second cards. To help, press on the left and
right sides of the box and the cards will spread a little.
The card will peek out at the notch. Put the box on the

table with the notch facing down so that the card is not visible.

Part II: Max draws the card
1. Hold the balloon dog with your right hand. Squeeze the box between the snout and the neck. Max drops the box.
2. Then repeat it, pushing the card that is sticking out in the notch 1 cm out of the box with your left thumb. The bubbles and the head grab the card. It holds on to it. When you lower the box, the card clings to the snout.

Max has pulled out the spectator's card. Bravo!

Tip:
To make it easier to slide the card out, cut an oval hole about 2 cm wide and 6 cm long on the side of the notch. If you hold the box in your left hand, you can push the card out with your thumb so that the balloon poodle can grab it more easily.

Be careful that the spectator does not see the opening! Always place the box on the table with the opening facing down.

Demonstration
Ask an assistant to come to you. Form a dog out of a balloon.
It's up to you whether it's already blown up or if you're still blowing it up.

Introduce Max, the balloon dog. Let the assistant draw a card, he remembers it and shows it to the audience. He returns the card to the pile.
Slide the pile back into the box that is on the table.
Hold Max. Hold the box against his snout. It falls down.
Say that Max is very excited. Talk him through it and try a second time. This time Max holds the card. He gets a round of applause.

The assistant gets to take Max home as a thank you gift. Say goodbye to your assistant and take a bow.

5. Magic games

If you're having a party, play magic games with your guests. Here are some suggestions:

Magic Wand Wars

One child is designated as the magician. He or she is given a magic wand. The children can move around in a marked out field.
The wizard must now try to enchant the children. This is done by touching the children with the wand. When he touches a child, the child have to stop immediately. He/she is petrified.
But they can be disenchanted by their fellow players. The still free teammates can crawl through the legs of the petrified child. Thus, the spell is lifted and the child may continue playing. The last free player may take over the role of the magician next, and the game starts again.

Zipp-Zapp

All the children sit in a circle of chairs. One of the partici-pants stands in the middle of the circle. There is no chair reserved for him. This person chooses a fellow player in the circle, goes to him and says, for example, "Zipp." The child addressed then says the name of his left neighbor.

But if he says "Zapp," he says the name of his right neighbor.

The third possibility is "Zipp-Zapp." Here all the children stand up and look for a new place.

The one who has not found a place must now continue the game. The game is over when everyone has had a good romp. There is no winner or loser.

Knock

All the children sit in a circle of chairs, close enough to put their left hand on their left neighbor's right knee and their right hand on their right neighbor's left knee. Get it? This is the starting point for the game.

The direction you choose is clockwise. You start. One by one, the hand is tapped once. This is not as easy as it sounds. It is easy to overlook the neighbor's hand that is in front of you in the row. Once everyone has under- stood, another variation is added. One has the possibility to knock twice in quick succession. Then the direction changes and it's the previous neighbor's turn again.

If someone has knocked incorrectly, he must take his hand out of the game. The winner is the one whose hand is the last one still in the game.

This game requires a high level of concentration, but is a lot of fun.

Game: Black Magic

This game is always amazing for all players. It is about clairvoyance. One child knows exactly which object the other teammates will choose.

The clairvoyant goes outside the door where she cannot hear the others. In the meantime, the children choose an object that is in the room, for example, a blue chair.

The psychic is invited in. Ask her about several objects. "Is it the red lamp?" The clairvoyant answers in the negative. "Is it the black box?" "No." "Is it the blue chair?" The clairvoyant answers in the affirmative.

Resolution: before the correct item is named, it is always preceded by a black item. So the item that follows it is the one chosen.

6. Appearance tips

Make up faces

With the help of make-up, people can look different. On stage, or in the theater, they can give more expression to the role they are slipping into. You don't always recognize a made-up face at first sight, but you do recognize the role it underlines, the one you're dressed up as, whether it's a robber, grandpa, animal, lion, or mouse. Children also love to put on makeup and look completely different. You can also use this tool for the magic show.

The only thing you need besides makeup is a steady hand and some imagination.

For the beginning or for bridging, the lipstick or kohl pencil from mother's make-up case is enough.

If you want to create more unusual make-up faces, you should get yourself some make-up utensils. You should use good brand make-up pencils or even choose a make-up box with several colors. Get a brush and sponge to apply the makeup.

Many children have sensitive skin or are prone to allergies. For this reason, it is advisable to get only really good makeup, as there is a risk that the cheap ones may contain allergens.

How everyone wants to look is up to each person and depends on the role the person is playing.

For example, the eyebrows can be changed to get a different expression. With a little makeup, your own brows are covered and the new brows are drawn in a different place. Or simply, the shape is changed.

If you paint a red dot in the corner of the eye next to the nose, the eyes will start to glow.

The face can be changed by adding a mustache. Or paint the lips and cheeks red so as not to look so pale in the spotlight.

After the performance, the makeup is removed. For this, paper tissues, grease cream and a mirror should be ready.

The grease cream is smeared all over the face. Everything is wiped off with the handkerchief. This can be repeated several times to get the face really clean. Then the face is washed off with soap and water.

Decorating for the performance

Create a magical ambiance before the performance. This is the icing on the cake. When the audience enters the room, they are overwhelmed by the bewitching aura. Balloons are a great decoration. You can hang them on the walls round the room.
Another option is to decorate the backdrop of the stage. To emphasize the edge of the stage, you can attach them to a string that hangs around the stage.

Another suggestion is that you paint a large picture, for which the maculature roll is suitable. You can use it as a stage background. Think about a magic motif that you can put on paper with paint.

You can make silhouettes. To do this, attach a large white sheet to the wall. Put a child in front of it and shine a lamp on it.

On the sheet you can see the shadow that represents the outline of the head. Trace the outline, and cut it out. Now use this as a template and place it on a black sheet, again tracing the outline and cutting it out. Already you have a perfect silhouette of an oversized head. The size depends on the format of your stage. As a guide-line, use about 30-40 cm. Vary the size by having the child whose head is being drawn move farther away or closer to the wall.

Balloon garlands as stage decoration

I recommend balloons as decoration. I'll introduce you to a method that takes a little time. Try it out beforehand. Use balloons with a diameter of 30 cm, which you inflate either with a balloon hand pump or, if available, an electric blower. Blow up all the balloons to the same size. You will need about 24 per meter.
- Tie 2 balloons together to form a pair, e.g. two white balloons and two balloons of a different color.

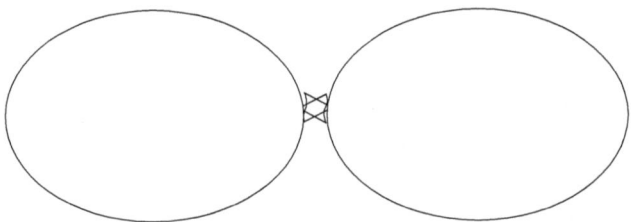

- Connect 2 pairs of balloons at the knotted point.

Place the pairs of balloons on top of each other. Turn balloons A and B so that they change places. Rotate them again so that they have reassumed their original positions. The balloons are now connected in the middle. The result is a four-leaf clover. This is our basic shape that we will continue to work with.

If you alternate the balloons in 2 colors you will get a spiral shape. You need seven to eight such "balloon cloverleaves" for one meter.

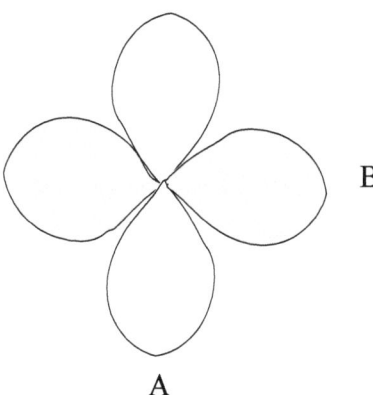

B

A

- Take a stable string, e.g. fishing line. Measure the length you want to decorate and add a meter at the beginning and at the end for fastening. Cut it.
Take these balloon clovers and knot the string around the middle. Place another cloverleaf on top of the first one so that the balloons are in the gap between them. Loop the string twice around the center of the second structure. It is now locked in place. The two clovers are attached to each other.

If you attach several of these balloon clovers to the rope on top of each other, it makes a great-looking garland that you can design according to your wishes, e.g. as an archway at the entrance, or as a stage decoration around the stage.

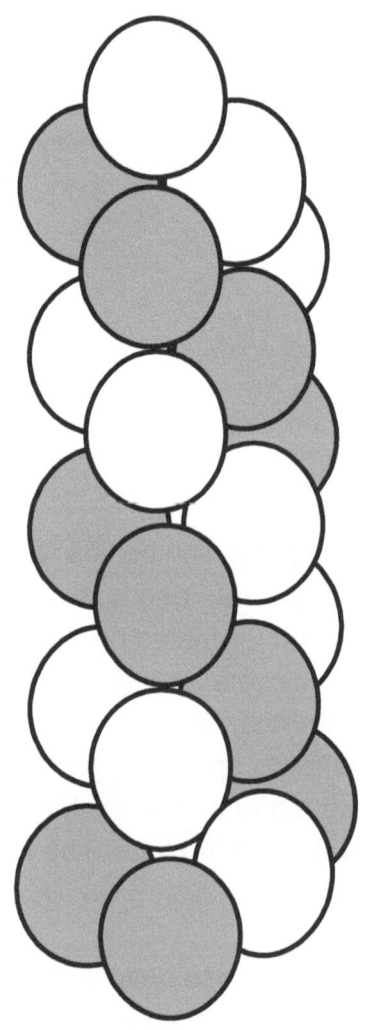

Visit me at Facebook

www.facebook.com/diezauberkiste

Look here for more free magic tricks:

www.die-zauberkiste.de

Magic moon

Since 1988, I have been working in Vellmar with my colleague Pia-B. Bluhm. Together we built up the group Zaubermond. Most of the young people there have been with us from the beginning.
We put on several magic programs and gave many performances regionally and nationally. We worked out many professional tricks. The children are bursting with self-confidence and developed a great momentum. Meanwhile, they give their own performances at children's birthday parties and children's festivals.

My Magic books

Susanne Rennert
Meine eigene Zaubershow
Bod

Susanne Rennert
Juchhu! Ich kann Geld zaubern
Bod

Ein kostenloses Zauberbuch bekommst du
bei www.zauberbuch.eu

- Lasse ein Papierei verschwinden und an einem anderen Ort wieder erscheinen.
- Zaubere ein zerschnittenes Seil wieder ganz.
- Zaubere aus einem 5 Euro Schein einen 10 Euro Schein.

Wie du das machst? Natürlich mit der Zaubertüte. Wie du sie bastelst erfährst du in diesem Buch.

Meine eigene Zaubershow

Komm mit in das Land der Magie. Erlebe die magische
Welt der Zauberei. Stelle die Naturgesetze auf den Kopf,
und lasse das Unmögliche Wirklichkeit werden. Dein
Publikum wird begeistert sein.
Wie werden Streichhölzer magnetisch?
Wie funktioniert der Lügendetektor?
Wie wird der Geist in der Vase lebendig?
Wie befreist du einen Ring?
Du erfährst die großen Zaubergeheimnisse. Lerne ver-
blüffende Zaubertricks und begeistere deine Freunde.
Fasziniere dein Publikum mit riesigen Seifenblasen.
Präsentiere deine eigene Zaubershow.
Erhältlich bei http://www.die-zauberkiste.de

Little Dino Donnie and his friends

By Danka Todorova

Get to know the little dino Donnie and his friends. You will experience some adventures with them. In several sequential stories, young readers can follow the exciting adventures. They will find many friends in places they will visit with their time machine. An incredible, simple and instructive story.

Thank you to the sponsors:

F&L Schulorganisation GmbH & Co KG
Neubeckumer Straße 39 a
59269 Beckum
www.schulorganisation.com

Heinrich Degenhardt
Brennstoffhandel GmbH & Co. KG
Hannoversche Str. 8
34266 Niestetal
www.heizoel-degenhardt.de

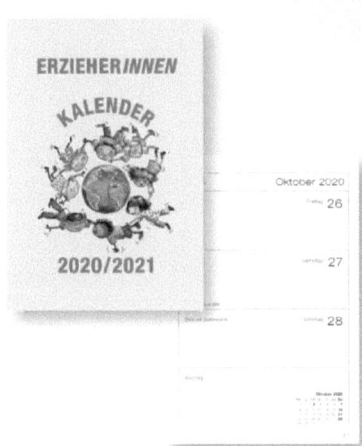